PIRANESI

PIRANESI

PIERRE SEGHERS

TRANSLATED BY IAN HIGGINS

FIRST PUBLISHED BY
FOREST BOOKS, 1993

20 Forest View, Chingford, London E4 7AY, UK
PO Box 312, Lincoln Centre, MA 01773, USA

First published in French under the title *Piranèse*,

Cover illustration: Piranesi, *Carceri d'invenzione*, Plate VI, State II (detail). This, and all other illustrations, reproduced by kind permission of the Ashmolean Museum, Oxford

Cover design: Ian Evans

British Library Cataloguing In Publication Data:
A catalogue record for this book is available from the British Library

ISBN: 1-85610-021-9

Typeset in Great Britain by Fleetlines Typesetters, Southend-on-Sea
Printed in Great Britain by BPCC Wheatons Ltd, Exeter

Introduction

In France, the name Pierre Seghers is inseparable from the idea of poetry. Almost invariably, however, people know of him not as a poet, but as a dynamic publisher and promoter of the work of other writers. But poet he was, and a considerable one. Although a concern with the contours of self underlies all his writing, his early poetry was often socially or politically oriented, and includes some powerful evocations of living, and dying, in occupied wartime France. With *Racines* (1956), however, he found what he himself rightly saw as his true voice. From then on, his poetry was a poetry full of questions, questions which, paradoxically, affirm the fragility and toughness of human creation. It is a poetry galvanised by three things: an obsessive awareness of the brevity of a human life; a realisation that this brevity makes life something even more miraculous, valuable and beautiful than we instinctively feel it to be; and a conviction that we only live this miracle to the full if we defend our freedom, and the freedom of others, to enjoy it. Seghers was someone who refused to live in the past (although a sense of the past pervades his work). One poem is entitled 'Vivre se conjugue au présent' ('The verb "to live" has only got a present tense'). Yet so essential is *language* to human beings that this man of action could also write, while daily risking his life in the Resistance, that 'il n'est de réel que de dire' ('the only reality is speech'). Hence this poetry that is itself resistance, resistance to the threat – and the temptation – of silence, immobility and resignation; a poetry of movement and change, of light brought into labyrinthine dark places.

Piranesi (1960), a single poem in twenty-seven short parts, epitomises these qualities. It is clearly marked by Seghers' Occupation experiences, by the post-war discovery of, and testimonies from, the Nazi concentration camps, and by the Communist regimes in Eastern Europe. But this political and historical awareness is integrated into a metaphysical, moral and aesthetic meditation on Piranesi's *Carceri* ('Prisons'). For thirty years, Seghers had been fascinated by these extraordinary engravings, which were for him revelations of an 'inner domain' of 'nightmarish fear' and 'indestructible hope'. In some ways, the poem emulates the engravings both thematically and formally. The sometimes stifling tension, the shifting chiaroscuro and lack of colour, the fragmentariness, the questions, the abrupt changes of direction, the false starts and dead ends, the prosodic hesitations between regularity and irregularity, the obstinate return to scrutinise and ponder each new arrangement of the prison – these are analogous to Piranesi's enigmatic figures, the lack of clear narrative, his combination of intricate realism with hallucinatory scales and perspectives, his often ambiguous light-source, the endless permutations of seemingly emblematic, but mysterious, objects that equip or decorate his vast dilapidated prisons. Although, unlike the *Carceri*, Seghers' poem perhaps slowly fights its way to something like an affirmation of hope, both the prints and the poem are exercises in dislocation and self-denial; Piranesi refuses the virtuoso architectural accuracy of which he was capable, Seghers refuses facile rhetoric or lyricism. In both – but more in the poem, perhaps – human genius is shown as blind and blinding, by turns entrapping itself in fantastic creations and dissolving them in fantastic light. Certainly, in the poem, the references to the speaker, to an unspecified woman or women and an unspecified man or men, and to humanity in general (which Seghers, like all French people of his generation, always refers to as 'l'homme' ('man')), ensure that the reflexivity introduced in the first part is never forgotten, Seghers' text referring to itself and the world outside itself as functions of one another. This combines with the references to theatre and ritual to reinforce the status of the poem as a myth, itself an intense ritual expression of the experience of good and evil. Indeed, the tight rhythmic and phonic control and steady build-up of tension and emotion in the poem do fit it particularly well for some kind of stylised public performance. (It was in fact staged at the Théâtre de la Ville in Paris, in 1983, with projections, dance, music by Roger Lahaye, and readings by Jean Mercure, Claude Giraux, François Maistre and Michel de Maulne.)

Pierre Seghers was born in 1906. When called up in 1939, he was stationed in the south and he saw no action. To do something useful, he started a soldiers' poetry magazine. After the Armistice in 1940, he relaunched the magazine as *Poésie*, intending to use it as a weapon against the Nazis and Vichy. *Poésie* became one of the main 'contraband' Resistance journals: to maximise the readership, it was published legally, so that any subversive material (and there was plenty) had to be 'smuggled in' in such a form that, while the censor could not object to it, the Resistance message would be clear to the alert reader. The review and the volumes published under its imprint functioned both as outlets for good poetry (Pierre Emmanuel and André Frénaud were among Seghers' 'discoveries') and as rallying cries, the editorial office becoming a Resistance headquarters. Meanwhile, Seghers was managing to write some poetry of his own as well as publishing other people's.

The farthest-reaching venture of the newly-created Editions Seghers was, in 1944, the 'Poètes d'aujourd'hui' series, a new concept in bringing poetry to a wide public in cheap, but well-produced, volumes, each with an introduction, photographs and a selection from the poet's work. In this and other series, Seghers published, often for the first time, over two thousand poets from all over the world.

In 1969, Seghers handed over his publishing house to Laffont, concentrating henceforth on a passionate campaign to awaken the poetry he believed to be dormant in everyone. He travelled indefatigably, in France and abroad, giving lectures and readings, organising discussions and debates. In 1975, he was awarded a doctorate by the University of Paris for a thesis on the place of poetry in contemporary society. While continuing to write his own poetry, he compiled anthologies, broadcast, made films, wrote a warning history of

French Resistance poetry, produced multi-media poetry evenings for the Théâtre de la Ville in Paris, and wrote French versions of Persian, Chinese and Turkish poetry. In 1983, he co-founded the Maison de la Poésie in Paris, and started a new poetry magazine the following year. Seghers was still working a fifteen-hour day until shortly before his death in 1987.

Poetry world-wide owes Pierre Seghers a great debt. Happily, although in France his own poetry is still in the shadow of his other activities, he has been translated into a number of languages – but not yet, apart from the odd short piece here and there, into English. We are glad to publish this bilingual edition of *Piranesi*, partly as a tribute to Seghers, and partly to widen the readership for a gripping text that puts challenging questions to our end-of-century world.

Giovanni Battista Piranesi (1720-1778) first trained as an architect and as a set-designer for the theatre. Although he is best known as an engraver, even his earliest works show both his mastery of intricate perspective architectural drawing and the influence of the spectacular oblique-perspective stage-sets popular in Italy at that time. He first made his reputation with views of Rome for tourists, and continued to produce these, and larger engravings of ancient Roman ruins, throughout his career. Seghers probably makes some allusions to the late engravings, notably those of the ruins of Paestum (1778), as well as to earlier works such as the 'Magnificent Port' (c. 1750). But the prime inspirations for the poem are the *Carceri d'invenzione* ('Imaginary Prisons', 1761), the augmented and heavily revised second edition of a set of etchings published in the late 1740s. It is for these sixteen prison scenes that Piranesi is most famous. There are no cells in these weird prisons. Most of the prisoners seem free to wander the galleries and endless complicated stairs of some ruinous, yet claustrophobic, Babel. Arches and pillars seen through arches, storey upon storey, grilles, spiked stakes, great iron rings, sinister hanging cages – or are they lanterns? – the mysterious, threatening paraphernalia combine with dizzying, sometimes impossible, perspectives and disturbing distortions of scale to create a nightmare atmosphere where even the screams of tortured men seem silent. Weirder still, some of the prisons are open to the outside world; yet the prisoners ignore it, still absorbed in soundless talk.

The technique of the *Carceri* contrasts greatly with that of Piranesi's exquisitely disciplined architectural prints. Thousands of nervous lines, as if the artist had stabbed manically at the plate, combine with massive shadows and swathes of light to heighten the unreal atmosphere. Although greatly reduced in size, the plates reproduced here do give some idea of Piranesi's genius. Seghers was not the first poet to find inspiration in that genius (Gautier and Hugo are among his predecessors): neither, surely, will he be the last.

Ian Higgins

The Translator

Ian Higgins was educated at Wyggeston Grammar School for Boys, Leicester, and at Exeter College, Oxford. Since 1966, he has taught in the French Department of the University of St Andrews, where he has been a Senior Lecturer since 1984. He has written extensively on modern French poetry. He has published a monograph on Francis Ponge and an edition of Ponge's *Le Parti pris des choses* (both London: Athlone Press, 1979), and an *Anthology of Second World War French Poetry* (2nd edition London: Routledge, 1991). Among his translations are a study of Chagall by André Verdet (*Chagall's World*, New York: Doubleday, 1984), and poems and fiction by French and Belgian writers in T. Cross (ed.), *The Lost Voices of World War I* (London: Bloomsbury, 1988). He is the co-author, with Sándor Hervey, of *Thinking Translation. A course in translation method: French-English* (London: Routledge, 1992). He is currently preparing an anthology of First World War French poetry.

Si la poésie ne vous aide pas
à vivre, faites autre chose.
Je la tiens pour essentielle à
l'homme, autant que les battements
de son coeur.

Si la poésie ne vous aide pas à vivre, faites autre chose. Je la tiens pour essentielle à l'homme, autant que les battements de son cœur.

Pierre Seghers

If poetry doesn't help you to live, do something else. In my view, it's as vital to human beings as their very heartbeat.

Pierre Seghers

Piranesi, *Carceri d'invenzione,* Plate IV, State II.

Piranesi, *Carceri d'invenzione*, Plate V, State I.

Piranesi, *Carceri d'invenzione*, Plate VII, State II.

Piranesi, *Carceri d'invenzione*, Plate XIV, State II.

PIRANESI

Pourtant, bien que chacun se fuie
Comme la prison qui le tient et le hait,
Il est un grand miracle dans le monde:
Je sens que toute vie est quand meme vécue.

R. M. Rilke, *Le Livre d'heures*
(tr. Lou Albert-Lasard)

And yet, though each runs fleeing from himself
As from the prison that holds and hates him,
There is a great wonder in the world,
I feel it: all life is *lived.*

R. M. Rilke, *The Book of Hours*

Je vous écris avec une encre sans pardon
pour la mémoire et le stylite. Une colonne et puis une autre
dressent un temple imaginaire où les nuages se défont.
Je vous écris d'une prison où sont les fosses si profondes
qu'on y devine entre les murs des escaliers sans fin, tournant
jusqu'au plus noir du noir comme au cœur du silence.
Je vous écris à voix posée comme un langage de captifs
pris dans leur solitude et plus grands, d'un abîme
d'où s'élève l'architecture des raisons,
des raisons folles, des tours de Babel, des idées
plantées dans l'eau et l'eau emporte leurs reflets.

I am writing to you in an ink
unforgiving to memory and stylite. One column, then another,
raise an imaginary temple where the clouds drift to nothing.
I write to tell of the prison I am writing from, where the dungeons
go so deep that endless stairs are sensed within the walls, winding
into blackest black, as if to the heart of silence.
I write, steady-voiced as captives gripped by solitude and greater for it,
of this abyss and the structure rising from it,
the constructed architecture of reasons,
insane reasons, towers of Babel, ideas
built on water, reflections washed away.

La nuit tombe. On dirait que des fanaux s'allument
dans les plombs des vitraux où saigne un feu. Ni l'or
du jour naissant, ni la lumière verticale
de midi, ne composent un tel orchestre. On y entend
d'une ville oubliée les bruits qui se dispersent,
un lointain grondement, une respiration
qui se tait, et le silence des abîmes
s'installe. Rien ici, personne ici, tout est absent
et qui donc veillerait? Nul fantôme ne vient
dans l'intérieure nuit où l'autre se repose
hanter ces escaliers, un épais rideau tombe
sur le théâtre et ses décors. Sombre sommeil
si pareil à la mort et comme elle, inutile...

Night is falling, stained glass bleeding fire
like beacons lighting in the leads. The gold
of day dawning, the light sheer overhead
at noon – neither puts such harmonies together. Sounds
come scattered from a forgotten city,
a murmur in the distance, breathing falling still,
and the silence of utter depth
settles in. Nothing here; no one here; only absence.
For who would keep vigil? No phantom comes
into the inner night the outer rests in
to haunt these stairs; a thick curtain is falling
round the theatre and its sets. Such gloomy sleep,
so very like death; and just as useless.

Et si c'était l'honneur, d'attendre sur ces marches
que le temps dégringole et si le temple obscur
annonçait des jardins éblouissants? Si l'ombre
traversée tout à coup d'éclairs se déchirait
pour révéler le jour promis? Il monte un air
de draps humides et de linceuls, mais l'homme lit
des inscriptions gravées dans les géométries
des appels insensés. Il hale avec des câbles
des fardeaux, des palais qu'il a construits pour lui,
plus grands d'être ruinés. Les lanternes aveugles
ne le concernent plus. Sous les cintres ouverts
lentement, il gravit les degrés et s'avance.

And what if this were honour, to wait on these steps
while time tumbled down them? and what if the temple
foreshadowed dazzling gardens? What if the dark
were shot through with sudden lightning and tore
to reveal the promised day? An air is rising
as of shrouds and damp cloth, but man reads
engraved inscriptions in the geometries
unreason gives voice to. With ropes, he hauls
dead weights, palaces he has built for himself,
now greater ruined. The blind lanterns
he can ignore now. Up through the open archways
he slowly climbs, further, step by step.

Le tribunal, où donc est-il? Dans la lumière sous les plombs
éventrés, là-bas au-delà des fenêtres
où se devine un soleil fou. Le tribunal, est-ce le ciel
qui voit chaque matin les hommes prisonniers
de leurs rêves, monter les degrés et descendre
la solennelle architecture des rumeurs?
Homme, temple béant où le cérémonial
s'affouille, forêts d'échos où l'innocent avoue
sous la herse et la roue, son attente. Il rêvait
de colonnes, de voûtes glorieuses, de pilastres,
de blocs appareillés pour se faire un château
dont il eût été Roi. Les charpentiers du ciel
ont planté le décor pour ses splendeurs, ses fêtes,
et dans le rare éclat du jour, il va, poussant
une brouette de silence, là où des larves
grouillent dans leur grandeur défunte, à ras du sol.

So where do they hold the court? In the light underneath
the ripped-open lead, beyond the windows
a crazy sun is hinted in. Is the court heaven, the sky
that every morning watches men imprisoned
by their dreams walk up the stairs and down
the ritual constructions of hum and mutter?
Man: a gaping temple of eroding
ceremonial, deep forests of echoes where,
underneath portcullis teeth and wheel, the innocent
confesses his patient wait. He was dreaming
of pilasters, columns, glorious vaulting
and ashlar cut to make himself a castle
where he would be King. The sky's own carpenters
have built the set for his festivals and splendour –
and on he goes, through fragments of daylight,
pushing a barrow of silence past ghosts teeming
grub-like in their dead grandeur, on the ground.

Etaient-ce les plaideurs d'une cause perdue
Ceux-là? Ils avaient choisi de vivre ici,
dans le désastre reconnu. La mort passait
chaque jour, mais des ruines ils relevaient des temples
où l'ombre devenait un feu. Ils surgissaient
ici et là, carriers, maîtres tailleurs de pierres et de paroles,
architectes d'une folie où s'émerveillait la raison,
bâtisseurs écrasés mais toujours redoutables,
vénérés et craints. Etaient-ce les plaideurs
d'une cause perdue ou étaient-ce nos juges
qui fouillaient de leurs yeux les reflets du miroir?

Were these the pleaders of a lost cause?
They had agreed, had chosen, to live here,
in full acknowledged disaster. Death passed
each day, but from the ruins they raised new temples
where fire was lit from darkness. They could appear
anywhere, quarrymen, master carvers of stones and speech,
architects of a madness reason marvelled in,
builders crushed but ever formidable,
venerated, feared. Were they the pleaders
of a lost cause, or were they our judges
probing the reflections in the mirror?

Si improbable était l'issue. Si souterraine
et creusée si profond la crypte, où le soleil
ne brillait que pour l'ombre. On écrasait un Dieu
sous le lourd appareil des pierres solennelles,
et si seul était-il qu'il ne se cherchait plus.
Il n'y avait rien de terrifiant dans cet abîme
organisé, mais de voûtes en vestibules
d'ogives en couloirs, de passages en degrés
on y respirait de plus en plus mal, comme suffoque
celui que son absence étrangle. On étranglait
le jour, la clarté du jour dans cette fosse
étrangement déserte et silencieuse. Comme
des ombres, quelques formes se calligraphiaient sur des
balustres,
aveuglées, se penchant sur le temps incertain
d'où montait une odeur d'encens pourri. Là-haut,
sous le berceau de la charpente et sous les dalles
de longs filins s'effilochaient. Mais au-delà
la lumière vibrait, bourdon sur le sépulcre
ouvert comme un vaisseau qu'abandonnaient les rats.

So unlikely was a way out. And dug
so deep underground the crypt, where the sun
shone only for dark shadow. Crushed under
the weighty ritual of stonework was a God
so alone he had given up the search for self.
There lurked no terrors in this orderly
abyss, but from arches to corridors,
from vaults to vestibules, from passageways to steps,
breathing grew ever harder, like the suffocation
of one choking on his absence. They choked
the day, the day's light, in this strangely empty,
silent pit of a dungeon. Like shadows,
a dim calligraphy of forms did gaze down from balustrades,
blinded, into the uncertainty of time
and catch its putrid incense. Overhead,
from the ceiling-timbers, from stone slabs,
long ropes hung fraying. But out beyond, a bell
of vibrant light was sounding, above the tomb
split open like a ship the rats abandon.

Il ne restait plus rien que les piliers porteurs
des voûtes colossales. Il ne restait plus rien
que l'ombre exorcisée, rien qu'une plaie de pierres
ouverte sur le pus des ténèbres. On voyait
toutes les charnières et les instruments du système
de la terreur, les dents plantées sur des épieus
dans un ordre dément. On voyait l'ordonnance
des lieux obscurs, les passerelles
qui butaient sur le vide et sur l'écrasement.
On y voyait le poids, la force,
et les secrets de la machine du pouvoir
surpris et dévoilés jusque dans leurs assises.
Ce n'était que cela. Les marches d'un palais,
un labyrinthe de silence
où nul n'osait parler, la nombreuse structure
faite pour pétrifier chacun avec chacun.

Nothing was left but the pillars that bore
the colossal vaults. Nothing was left
but darkness exorcised, a scab of stones split open
to the putrefying gloom. Through it
showed the crucial instruments of systematic
terror, the spiked shafts and iron in ordered
lunacy. Through it, all the architecture
of the shadows showed, the catwalks
ending in empty space and men smashed.
Through it showed weight, and force,
the secrets of the machinery of power
discovered and stripped down to the bedrock.
That was all it was. Some palace steps,
a labyrinth of silence
none dared speak in, the multiple structure
created to petrify each man with each.

Punir? Mais qui punir? Et de quoi? D'être libre
d'aimer le vin qui coule et la femme amoureuse,
de préférer le jour à la nuit, le soleil
aux disciplines, aux macérations de l'amertume
Punir... Ils aimaient punir et enfoncer
le visage des prisonniers dans la poussière
des temps passés. Ils le courbaient, l'agenouillaient,
faisaient la nuit dans sa mémoire,
le rendaient pauvre, la bouche pourrie par un péché
qu'ils inventaient. Ils étaient les bourreaux de l'âme,
parfaitement secrets et pleins d'onction. On les eût dit
charitables, ils étaient froids comme une lame.
Ils ne tuaient pas. Ils volaient la vie de chaque instant
Chaque brin d'herbe devenait leur soldat, mais la chaleur
des mains, qu'en faisaient-ils? A se prosterner sur les
marbres
toute vie se perdait, le cœur devenait froid.

Punish? But whom? And why? For being free
to love flowing wine and a woman in love,
to prefer day to night, the sunshine
to steeping in some harsh and penitential bitterness.
Punish... They loved punishing, and forcing
prisoners' faces down into the dust
of times passed. They made them kneel and bow the head,
made darkness in the memory
and made them poor, inventing sins that rotted out
the mouth. They were the torturers of the soul,
consummately secret, full of unction. They might
have been thought charitable: they were blade-cold.
They did not kill. They stole the light from every moment,
every stalk of grass turned soldier for them – but what did
they do
about the warmth of hands? Once prostrate on carved
marble,
any life was lost, the heart turned cold.

Peut-être un feu grégeois, peut-être une fumée
pour des fers à rougir, peut-être un accident,
un instant de tumulte dont on attend qu'il passe,
une stridence, une dissonance, un éclat
pour rompre l'ordre et l'harmonie, une folie,
un Cri. Aurait-on entendu un Cri? Ni les guetteurs, ni les
passants,
ni les indifférents qui causent dans les salles,
ni l'ouvrier sur son échelle, ni le promeneur attardé
sur l'encorbellement du temps, n'ont entendu.
De quoi s'agissait-il? D'un cri... Mais le cri passe
pour la gloire de la durée, pour une pierre dans un mur
sur une autre pierre scellée. Un machiniste
s'était-il trompé? C'était une erreur. Pas même un cri...

Perhaps a gleam of Greek fire; or smoke from iron
coming to red heat; or an accident,
a moment's turmoil that 'will soon be over',
something shrill, discordant, jagged-loud to break
the harmony and order, something mad,
a Cry. Might someone have heard a Cry? Not the
watchmen, nor the passers-by,
nor those conversing unmoved in the great halls,
nor the workman on his ladder, nor the lingering stroller
still
up on the balconies of time – none heard.
What was it, then? A cry... But a cry passes,
to the glory of duration: a stone in a wall keyed in
with another stone. Had a stage-hand gone wrong
somewhere? It was all a mistake. Not even a cry...

Mais dans un songe de palais, pour quels synodes, pour
quels drames
cet enchevêtrement d'ombres et de lueurs,
cet appareil de la fortune où les offices
sont comme un châtiment? La fable qui ordonne
de la tore au larmier un édifice fou
est à la gloire des jardins, de la lumière.
L'homme échappe à ses monstres, les châteaux inventés,
il les incarcère dans des salles
où l'absence les prend. La rampe, le rideau
ne dissimulaient rien. Chevalets et carcans
les voici dévoilés. Les conspirations
perdent sens et substance, et se dénouent. Enfin
le calme...

But why, in a dream of palaces, for what synod, what
  dramas,
this entanglement of glints and shadows,
this ritual construct of fortune where worship
is like a punishment? From plinth to drip
the whole mad pile is structured by a fable
glorifying gardens and the light.
Man escapes his monsters – invents the castles,
imprisons them in great halls
where they are seized with absence. Footlights, curtain –
these were masking nothing. The whipping-posts
and racks stand here exposed. The conspiracies
unravel, lose all sense and substance. Perfect
peace, at last...

Comme un homme entravé, noué dans ses cordages,
Il regardait les fûts énormes, et livré
à celui qui sculptait la pierre et la durée,
Il s'étonnait d'être si peu. Mais dans la carrière, les blocs
Il les avait domptés et charriés jusqu'à lui
et, pour exorciser ses rêves fantastiques
Il avait fait surgir des lions des profondeurs.
Au-dessus de lui, c'était le chaos et son ordre,
des licteurs en surplomb, des poutres suspendues
sur l'intraitable effort des déraisons. Le temple,
par le ciel habité accueillait le soleil
pour une dilection d'éclats et de ténèbres.
Lui n'était rien. Pas même un visage. Il n'était
qu'un lien pour attacher des hommes à des pierres
et pour hisser plus haut les lourds anneaux de fonte
où viendraient coulisser les câbles de son treuil.

Like a man trapped and tangled in his ropes,
he stared at the huge columns, and bondsman now
to the sculptor of stone and duration
was shocked to find himself so slight. But, in the quarry, he
had tamed
the blocks – overpowered them, dragged them to him,
and, to exorcise fantastic dreams,
had conjured lions from the depths.
Above him was chaos and its order,
lictors looking down, beams hanging over
the intractable strivings of unreason.
The temple, sky-filled, bade welcome to the sun,
for pure love of darkness and splintering light.
He was nothing. Not even a face. He was
just a rope for binding men to stones
and hoisting higher the great cast-iron rings
his winchgear cables were to run through.

Quelles fourmis infatigables, quelles fourmis
creusent ici cette prison de la lumière
qui évide le temps, et fait de ses tunnels
un énorme château de voûtes et de chaînes?
Quelles fourmis infatigables, quelles fourmis
l'une à l'autre liées se dépensent, se pressent
pour bâtir un château? On voit des théories
descendre lentement l'escalier du Prince
et d'autres n'apporter que du vent, convertir
le vide en monument d'échos. Qui donc habite
cette caverne? Qui transforme tout ce qu'il touche?
Qui fait un geste et fait se lever le soleil
sur l'illumination des socles dans les têtes?
Et ceux-là, que contemplent-ils? En eux, l'obscur
devient clarté, en eux le chaos s'organise,
la fureur et le bruit se font ordre. L'on dit
qu'ils ont fait du néant un temple imaginaire
qui ne peut plus mourir.

What indefatigable ants, what gangs
of ants are digging this prison of the light
that hollows out time and from its tunnels
is making one huge castle of vaults and chains?
What indefatigable ants, what gangs
of ants are straining so and thronging so
to build a castle? Solemn files are seen
processing slowly down the Prince's stair,
while others bring empty air, elaborating
echoes out of emptiness. So who lives
in this cavern? Who changes all he touches?
Who simply motions and makes the sun rise
on the plinths lit up inside men's minds?
– And those contemplatives, what can they see? In them
dark turns to light, chaos becomes pattern,
sound and fury, order. They are said to have made
from the void an imaginary temple
that cannot die now.

Aux lucarnes, des grilles. Des grilles aux fenêtres,
dans le cintre des baies, des grilles. Aux balcons,
des grilles. Et cependant nulle prison n'existe
ici, mais un palais donnant sur des jardins.
Les murs ne se voient plus. Ici même, les portes
ont disparu. Dans un cauchemar de verrous
l'Ordre est né. C'est le royaume de l'arcade
ouverte sur le ciel et sa coupole bleue.
Qui parlait de captifs, d'esclaves, de Sisyphe?
Ils ont fait un château de l'inutilité
pour rien, pour le plaisir, le bonheur de suspendre
chaque jour un balcon plus haut pour s'accouder
Et qui s'évaderait? Les grilles dérisoires
empêchent-elles le ciel d'entrer comme chez lui
ici, où les flambeaux ne projettent plus d'ombre?

Across the skylights, bars. Bars at the windows,
bars across the arched bays. Bars along
the balconies. And yet there is no prison
here, but a palace giving onto gardens.
No walls are seen now. From this very place
the doors have vanished. In a nightmare of bolts
Order has appeared. It is this kingdom
of archways open to the sky's blue dome.
Who spoke of Sisyphus and slaves and captives?
They have made a castle of uselessness,
for nothing, for the pleasure, each day, of raising
a still higher balcony to lean from.
And who would escape? Do these paltry bars
stop the sky filling this place and settling
here, where the torch-flames cast no shadow now?

Est-ce déroute ou bien chantier? On érige dans les arcanes
un labyrinthe de grandeur où la lumière s'épaissit,
un rêve de forêts où la pierre s'anime
dans l'enchevêtrement des chaînes et des liens.
Qui a taillé ces lions, quels devins ou quels hommes
ont jeté vers le ciel les arches de ces ponts,
suspendu ces poulies pour ne soulever rien?
Un jeu de vides et de prodiges
s'accomplit là toujours plus haut, sans autre but
que de bâtir dans l'air un palais gigantesque,
de s'affairer à des travaux où la montagne et le rocher
surgiront de la main. Suspendus, les jardins
seront d'un ordre ingrat auprès des temples. Herses,
Esclaves enchaînés cernés dans la lumière,
Passé recomposé qui regardez toujours
les peines et les jeux devenir des colonnes,
que pensez-vous de nous? Notre prison respire...

Collapse and chaos, or a building site? In mysteries of
construction
there is rising a labyrinth of grandeur where the light
thickens,
a dream of forests where stone comes to life
among entanglements of chain and rope.
Who carved these lions, what visionaries or what men
threw the arches of these bridges skyward
and hung these pulleys to hoist nothing?
Prodigious interactions of empty space and exploit
are in play, higher, higher still, with no aim
but to build a giant palace in the air,
to bustle and labour to conjure mountain and rock
from human hands, and temples of greater grace
even than hanging gardens. Portcullises
and slaves in chains caught pallid in the light –
you, the reassembled past still watching
the pain and toil and play turn into pillars,
how do you think of us? Our prison breathes...

Dans un péristyle de lanterneaux et d'échauguettes,
dans un palais de ponts-levis et de gibets,
Silence. L'ombre ne règne pas ici, mais la lumière
d'un jour toujours semblable et neuf. On n'entend pas
les pas des visiteurs, ni les voix, ni la rose
du temps s'ouvrir, mais on écoute à l'intérieur
un orchestre de blancs et de noirs et de lignes,
une chorégraphie monumentale, ballet du Prince de la
grandeur.
Chaque jour enfermé, à chaque jour plus libre,
à chaque jour plus mort et toujours plus vivant,
plus misérable et plus royal, éternel condamné mais encore
sursitaire,
absent mal délivré, opprimé mais unique,
sous de plus hautes voûtes, un homme.

In a peristyle of turrets and lantern-lights,
in a palace of drawbridges and gibbets,
Silence reigns – and not darkness, but a daylight
ever the same and new. None hear the footfall
of callers, or voices, or the rose of time
opening; but, inside, counterpoints of lines
in whites and blacks are heard and listened to,
a monument in choreography, the Prince of grandeur's
grand ballet.
Every day shut in, each day more free,
each day more dead and ever more alive,
more pitiful and more kingly, for ever sentenced but his
sentence still suspended,
absent unreleased, oppressed but unique,
under higher vaults, a man.

Si loin, la gloire des colonnades sous des arches,
les jeux recomposés du jour. Ici, la nuit
sous de sombres portiques. Là-haut, la frise où se retrouve
l'homme ivre d'être heureux. Des chaînes, en dessous,
énormes, et des pals, des ancres et des roues
dans l'intérieur obscur d'un dédale couvert
de plombs. Celui qui fête son triomphe
n'est pas un évadé, il invente le sol
et le jaillissement des forêts de colonnes.
Au seuil de sa folie, une lanterne noire,
la raison comme un fil à plomb sans emploi. Le soleil
est sa seule sagesse, il vit et il dispose
l'inutile attirail en un agencement.
Ce n'est pas à l'assaut du ciel qu'il grimpe, mais de
  lui-même,
Entrepreneur d'illuminations, artificier du plein midi
quand sa victoire éclate et devient un nuage
que le vent des lointains disperse et réunit.

So far off through arches, the glory of colonnades,
the play and rearrangements of daylight. Here,
leaden night, in porticoed gloom. Overhead, the frieze that
shows
the happy luck-drunk their reflection. Below,
chains, huge, and stakes, anchor-irons and wheels
deep inside the darkness of a maze roofed
with lead. A man who celebrates his triumph
is no escapee – he is inventing
the soil for forests of columns to spring from.
At the threshold of his madness, a black lantern,
reason like a plumbline hanging idle. The sun
is his sole wisdom; it lives, it sorts the useless
clutter into organised equipment.
It climbs in conquest, not of the sky, but of itself,
switcher-on of lighting, setter-off of fireworks at noon
when its victory explodes into a cloud
dispersed and recomposed by the far wind.

Echafaudages qui touchez au ciel, que les nuées
traversent, lourds piliers
pour ne rien soutenir que des voûtes occultes
sur des cintres béants, gradins, vastes degrés
qui ne menez à rien, je vous salue. Sans vous,
nul élargissement, l'épaisseur et l'opaque.
D'une prison, celui qui construit un palais
pour le compte d'un roi est un roi. Son empire
est son temple intérieur. Ses fastes et ses fêtes
sont ses géométries par ses rêves habitées.

Constructions scaffolded sky-high, drifted through
by clouds, heavy pillars built
to bear nothing but hidden archways high
over openings, huge steps, stairways climbing
up to nothing: I salute you. Without you
is no breadth, no release; thickness, opaqueness.
The man who, from a prison, builds a palace
for a king, is a king. His empire: the temple
inside him. His pomp and celebration:
the geometries he frames and lets his dreams fill.

Mais, au-delà des plombs, le ciel. Mais au-delà
des frontons et des toits, le ciel. Et sur le faîte
toute mort dépassée, le ciel. Un univers
roule autour d'un moyeu géant, comme une roue,
et l'homme qui vivait de soleils en prisons,
inventait. La fin n'était pour lui qu'une ombre un peu plus
  noire
d'où la lumière surgissait. Une magnificence
de quartiers de pierre s'édifiait
sur un cloaque devenu poussière de silence,
et nulle déraison n'atteignait la grandeur
de la transparence infinie...

But, beyond all the lead, the sky. And beyond
the pediments, the sky. And over the roofs,
outdistancing all death, the sky. A universe
turns wheeling round a giant hub, and the man
who lived a life of suns and prisons was
an inventor. To him, the end was just a rather blacker
shadow
the light sprang from. Magnificence made stone
rose in edifices over
sinks of filth that were now dust, dust and silence;
and there was no unreason to touch the grandeur
of the infinite transparence.

Dans les gravois et les décombres, dans les dépôts de matériaux
de démolition, dans un cimetière de vestiges
Ce qu'il faut : Des blocs bien jointoyés pour dresser les piliers
d'une demeure éblouissante, verticale.

Dans le supplice et le chagrin, dans un domaine de serrures,
Dans les hasards et les cellules, dans les cages de la torpeur,
Ce qu'il faut : Des fondations énormes qui demeurent
pour supporter le poids du ciel, le poids du temps.

Dans le tumulte et le désordre, dans l'écheveau inextricable
des questions sans réponse et du parler tout seul
Ce qu'il faut : un rêve vigilant offert à la lumière
Et le palais secret ouvert à tous les vents.

In the ruins and the debris, in the spoil-heaps
of demolition, in a cemetery of hints and traces
are needed these: dressed blocks, flush-pointed, to raise
high pillars
for a sheer and dazzling habitation.

In the torture and suffering and grief, in a realm of locks,
in chance and hazard and prison cells, in the cage of
lethargy
are needed these: enormous foundations put down to last,
to take the double weight of sky and time.

In the din and disorder, in the inextricable ravel
of questions without answer and talk to self
are needed these: a waking, watchful dream offered to the
light,
the secret palace open to every wind.

Dans la prison du sage un or se multiplie
qui ressemble aux reflets du soleil sur une eau
fuyant au long du temps. Un or qui se disperse
en rayons, en regards et en complicité
silencieuse. Les bruits lointains qui retentissent
n'arrivent plus ici. Dans la tour du Savoir
un feu fera du Rien le déambulatoire
qui va de porche en porche et reconduit au Rien.
Mais qu'importe. Un feu éclaire la durée,
Il illumine le passage, il fait une vie de plain-chant
dans le pays des pas-perdus. Et une lampe
suffit à la rançon, mais nul n'est détenu.

In the wise man's prison is a gold prolific
as reflections of the sun on water
and the flight of time. A gold that scatters
into rays of light and looks of silent
collusion. Distant sounds no longer echo
here. In the tower of Knowledge, a fire
will make from Nothingness the aisle that leads round
from porch to porch and back to Nothingness.
But what of it. A fire illuminates
duration, lights up the to and fro of waiting, makes a life of
plainsong
in the endless ante-land. And a lamp
is ransom enough, but there is no prisoner.

Sur le fond noir luisent des taches de lumière,
Une poursuite ou un ballet. Il y a aussi un homme en croix
qu'on ne voit pas, ses genoux s'affaissent et il se tourne
vers l'ange devenu guerrier. Ses bras n'implorent pas, ils
   donnent,
Il chancelle et s'envole, il tombe et il s'en va.
Dans la clarté qui le délivre, il est plus grand que les
   ténèbres,
Etait-il prisonnier des lieux, habitait-il
cet enfer de murs-maîtres? Comme un roi sur un trône
il reçoit à présent les châsses transparentes
dans le narthex de la lumière. Un prêtre écoute sous l'étole
des mots qu'il n'entend pas et déjà le désert.

Against the background black there are brilliant glints –
a chase or a ballet. There is also a man on a cross,
unseen; his knees are sagging and he is twisting
towards the angel turned warrior; arms not suppliant, but
giving;
he stumbles and soars, he falls, and goes his way.
In the bright light that sets him free, he stands greater than
the dark.
Did he live here, cornered in, prisoner
to this hell of walls? Like a king enthroned now
he receives offerings of transparent shrines
in the narthex of the light. Listening, a stoled priest hears
words
he cannot grasp, and already the desert.

Sur le chemin de ronde, qui veille? La lumière,
et qui, derrière les barreaux? La lumière encore, il fait si
clair
que l'ombre perd son homme ici et qu'elle traîne
çà et là, comme aveuglée par la splendeur.
Non, ce n'est pas terrible ici, mais une fête,
Pas une crypte, mais un navire de haut bord
qui, avec nous, s'en va. Là-haut, on appareille
et la machinerie silencieuse s'entend
à peine. Déjà, on vogue en pleine mer.
Que rapporterez-vous des lointaines contrées
qui soit plus merveilleux? Quel haschich, quels alcools
vous donneront ces rêves? Et quelle architecture
au port vous attendra, qui les vaille? Rêvez...

Round the parapets, who is on watch? The light;
and who behind the bars? Again the light; it is so light here
that shadows lose their men and lie stranded,
floundering as if blinded by the splendour.
No, here is no terror, but a festival,
no crypt, but a towering ship leaving
with us. Up on deck they are casting off
and the silent engines are barely heard.
Already we are out at sea.
What shall you bring back from distant lands
that is more marvellous? What hashish, what liquor
shall give you these dreams? What seaport shall you find
with architecture to match them? Dream... dream...

Ils vivaient là parmi les trophées et les chaînes,
Passagers en transit et seuls, et gravissant
des marches, des degrés, des paliers, des échelles,
toujours plus haut, et silencieux. La nuit des temps
s'entrouvrait un instant pour eux. Ils venaient ajouter leur pierre,
non pas esclaves, mais libérés. Leur place était dans leur maison,
chantier toujours ouvert et plus vaste qu'eux-mêmes.
Ainsi, venus de loin, ils allaient, s'étonnant
des hauts portails ouverts, des murailles énormes
qu'ils agençaient sans le savoir. La lumière qui les guidait
s'appelait liberté...

There they lived, among the trophies and the chains –
travellers-through, and alone, and climbing
steps, stairs, landings, ladders, higher,
higher still, and silent. The mists of time
lit open for them briefly sometimes. Each came bringing a
stone,
not slaves, but freed men. Their place was in their own
house, an ever-open
building site much greater than themselves.
Thus they went – amazed, for all their journeying,
by the high, open portals, and the huge walls
they were skilfully, and unwittingly, constructing. The light
that led them
was called freedom…

Mais que font-ils là-haut derrière les attiques,
Animateurs de ce théâtre? Dans les souterrains de la nuit,
les travaux des légions qu'ils ne voient plus. Ils causent
et contemplent. Ce décor est leur ciel
leur œuvre, leur richesse, leur permanent prodige.
Ils n'ont pas l'air de s'être enfuis. A l'aise, ils sont
sur le sommet du praticable, ils ont la grâce
d'échapper au poids, de considérer la pesanteur
comme un cadre pour un miroir. L'obscurité
ceint le jour à venir, l'ombre n'est qu'un relief
de l'aube. A chaque jour
l'opéra se poursuit...

But what do they do, up among the rafters,
the producer-prompter-stagehands in this theatre? In
subterranean night
toil legions they no longer see. They converse,
and contemplate. This set is their sky,
their wealth – their own, their permanent, worked wonder.
They seem no fugitives. They move with ease
and grace on the summits of the feasible,
escaping weight, treating gravity as nothing more
than a frame for a mirror. The dark is wrapped
in the day to come, shadow just a cast shape
of dawn. With each day
the opera goes on...

Ce n'est pas une ébauche, un soupçon, un nuage,
ni ouï-dire, ni complot. Ce sont les signes
d'un trésor, ou bien les chiffres d'un langage
secret. N'entre pas ici qui le veut. On y apprend
à lire, à déchiffrer, à pénétrer. On entre
dans un monde lourd et trapu. On y apprend
à voir. On y découvre des vestibules,
des escaliers et des couloirs. On y apprend
le sens du labyrinthe et à toucher les pierres
qui faisaient peur. Mais dans un silence habité
une odeur de soleil s'installe. Chacun s'élève
lentement et va de palier en palier
toujours plus haut, là où les salles sont plus vastes,
On y apprend encore. Comme au-delà des murs
le chantier se poursuit, galeries et corniches
conduisent jusqu'au seuil qu'il faut franchir. Après,
on y apprend toujours à déchiffrer, à lire.

Here is no sketch, no surmise, no hint or cloud,
no hearsay, no intrigue. These signs mark
treasure, or are the cyphers of a secret
language. Uncommon, those who enter here. Here they
learn
to read, decypher, penetrate. They enter
a squat, dense, heavy world. Here they learn
to see. Here they discover vestibules,
and flights of stairs and corridors. Here they learn
where the labyrinth leads, and to touch the stones
that struck fear. But, in a lived-in silence,
the scent of sun settles in. They each climb
slowly up, landing by landing, higher,
higher still, to where the halls are greatest,
and there still they learn. The site continuing
beyond the walls, the galleries and ledges
lead to the threshold they must cross. Thereafter
still they learn to decypher, to read.

Sur ses tonneaux, Bacchus écoute le vin bruire
et crépiter le ciel. L'été s'est accoudé
à la vendange faite et le regarde. Il rêve...
Des vieillards le reçoivent, à genoux. Il est mort,
on le porte, il chavire
comme un grand mât vivant sur la houle. On l'accueille
pour des funérailles de Roi. Ses reins sont drapés de vin
doux.
Il était assis hier, ni dieu, ni faune
sous l'olivier. Un ange jouait du violon
près de lui, il entendait mûrir l'olive
et tourner le soleil sur sa vigne et son corps.
Avait-il dansé? Ou bien sa toison dévêtue
s'était-il mis plus nu qu'un marbre? Il ne savait
plus rien, il n'était plus là, sur des portiques
on taillait chaque jour ses rêves qu'en riant
d'un revers de sa main il effaçait pour d'autres...

Bacchus sits listening to his casked wine roar
and the crackling sky. Summer, elbows on
the finished vintage, leans watching him. He dreams...
Old men receive him, kneeling. He is dead,
he is carried, swaying like
a living mast tall on the waves. He is
made welcome for a kingly funeral. His loins are draped in
sweet wine.
Yesterday, no god or faun, he was sitting
under an olive-tree. An angel violin
played close by. He could hear the olives ripen
and the turning sun on his vines and his body.
Had he danced? or, casting off his fleece, stripped
more naked than carved marble? He remembered
nothing now, was gone now, and on porticos
each day they engraved his dreams, that with a laugh
and a flourish he wiped away, old for new...

Je vous écris au temps des plantes dans les ruines,
au temps du lierre et du figuier parmi des dalles de safran
où les colonnes sont éparses, brisées et couchées dans la
boue.
On a crevé le toit du temple et le soleil, qu'éclaire-t-il?
Une jachère arborescente où les fougères et les hommes
rêvent et meurent et vont de degrés en degrés.
Dans le lit d'une cannelure par cent mille mains évidée
dort un chien qui s'épuce et de grands pans de nuit
tombent sur les arceaux où les chardons bourdonnent,
et nul vent. Mais on entend, comme l'écho
d'une voix reconnue. Ecoute, le temps passe...

I am writing in the time of plant-grown
ruins, the time of fig-tree and ivy among saffron slabs,
with the fallen columns lying, snapped and scattered, in the
mud.
And through the broken-open temple roof, what does the
sun light up?
A rambling, ramifying, fallow place where ferns and men
dream, and die, and move on and up, step by step.
Bedded down in fluting hollowed by a million hands
a dog nuzzles fleas; widths of night fall in like walls
round arches buzzing with thistles; and no wind.
But, like the echo of a voice remembered,
there is a sound.
Just listen: time passing...

Select Bibliography

Pierre Seghers

Piranèse has been published in two editions. The first was published by Editions Ides et Calendes (Neuchâtel) in 1960. The text was slightly revised before republication in a volume which comprises the great majority of Seghers' published verse up to 1978: *Le Temps des merveilles* (Paris: Seghers, 1978). It is this text that, with one correction of an obvious misprint and another correction indicated by Seghers in 1987,* is reproduced in the present edition. An Italian translation of *Piranèse*, by R. Lucchese, was published in 1986, in *Villa Medici : Journal de voyage*, 1 anno, 0 (maggio 1986), pp. 43-54. After *Le Temps des merveilles*, Seghers' principal volumes of verse have been:

Commediante (Paris: Anke Kerlo, 1984)
Fortune Infortune Fort Une (Paris: Seghers, 1984)

Among Seghers' versions of foreign poetry are the following:

Saadi, *Gulistan ou le Jardin des roses* (Paris: Seghers, 1976)
Hâfiz, *Le Livre d'or du Divan* (Paris: Seghers, 1978)
Le Livre d'or du haïkaï [with Cl. Gertler] (Paris: Laffont, 1984).

Most of Seghers' songs are collected in two volumes of *Chansons et complaintes* and two of *Nouvelles chansons et complaintes*, all published by the Editions Seghers between 1958 and 1964. Many of these songs have been recorded by such artists as Jacques Douai, Léo Ferré, Juliette Gréco, Serge Kerval and Hélène Martin; for fuller details see the discography in *Le Temps des merveilles*. Seghers' other writings include the following:

Clavé, (Barcelona: Polígrafa, 1974)

---

*In conversation with Mary B. Rigby, to whom I am indebted for the information.

La Résistance et ses poètes [second edition; 2 volumes] (Verviers: Nouvelles Editions Marabout, 1978)
Louis Jou, architecte du Livre et des Baux (Paris: Poppy Jou et Pierre Seghers, 1980)
Monsu Desiderio, ou le théâtre de la fin du monde (Paris: Laffont, 1981)
Victor Hugo visionnaire (Paris: Laffont, 1983).

Seghers compiled a number of anthologies, in addition to a major selection of Resistance poetry in *La Résistance et ses poètes*. Notable among these are:

Le Livre d'or de la poésie française contemporaine [2 volumes] (Verviers: Nouvelles Editions Marabout, 1969)
Le Livre d'or de la poésie française des origines à 1940 [2 volumes] (Verviers: Nouvelles Editions Marabout, 1972)
*Anthologie des poètes maudits du XX*e *siècle* (Paris: Belfond, 1985)

Helpful works on Seghers are:

Pierre Seghers par l'auteur (Paris: Seghers, 1973)
C. Seghers, *Pierre Seghers: un homme couvert de noms* (Paris: Laffont, 1981)
Poésie 88, No. 21 (janv.-févr. 1988); this issue is a tribute to Seghers, and includes much material by and on him.
M. B. Rigby, *The Poetry of Pierre Seghers*, unpublished PhD. thesis (University of St. Andrews, 1988). This thesis contains the fullest bibliography yet compiled of work by and on Seghers.

Piranesi

The following books are good studies of Piranesi, and include reproductions of the *Carceri*:

A. Robison, *Piranesi: Early Architectural Fantasies* (Washington, U.S.A.: National Gallery of Art, 1986)
J. Scott, *Piranesi* (London: Academy Editions, 1975)
J. Wilton-Ely, *The Mind and Art of Giovanni Battista Piranesi* (London: Thames and Hudson, 1978)

Further French Poetry from Forest Books

Modern French Poetry
Selected & Translated by Martin Sorrell
Introduced by Lawrence Sail

A vibrant anthology bringing together the individual voices of eleven very different poets, and reflecting the breadth and energy of twentieth-century French poetry. Established figures rub shoulders with comparative newcomers (even in France) many of whom have never before been translated into English. Dual Text French/English.

Includes: Anne-Marie Albiach, Marie-Claire Bancquart, Danielle Collobert, Jean Daive, Robert Desnos, Louise Herlin, Philippe Jaccottet, Pierre McOrlan, Joyce Mansour, Jacques Prévert, Jules Supervielle.

1-85610-005-7 pbk £9.95

Sleepwalker with Eyes of Clay
Jean-Jacques Celly

New prose poems from the contemporary French poet, novelist and essayist. Translated by Katherine Gallagher.

1-85610-029-4 pbk £5.95 published November 1993

Baudelaire's Paris
Edited & Translated by Laurence Kitchin

Poems by Baudelaire, Verlaine, Nerval and Juan Ramón Jiménez reacting to the nineteenth-century urban nightmare. New English translations side-by-side with the original French and Spanish.

0-948259-97-3 pbk £3.95

Love Sonnets of the Renaissance
Edited & Translated by Laurence Kitchin

Poems by Ronsard, Du Bellay, Petrarch, Castiglione and Garcilaso de la Vega in new English translations side-by-side with the original French, Italian, Spanish and Portuguese.

0-948259-60-4 pbk £6.95